I0164370

Should I
Wait
in Faith
or # Step Out
in Faith?

Balancing Patience
and Initiative
in the Christian Life

M. Blaine Smith

SilverCrest
B•O•O•K•S

Library of Congress Control Number: 2013900071

ISBN: 978-0-9840322-8-0

Contents

Author's Note

I am pleased to have the opportunity in this short book to expand on an article I wrote some time ago for my *Nehemiah Notes* series, and have included as a chapter in two previous books. We wrestle with the question of whether to wait in faith or step out in faith probably more than any other in the Christian life. Fortunately, the most basic answer to this question is a simple principle, which I present in chapter one. But more needs to be said about how this principle applies to the real-life situations and challenges we face in our Christian walk, and we'll look at these critical areas in the other chapters.

There's no question that we Christians tilt too greatly toward being passive, and not enough toward taking serious initiative, to solve our problems, find answers to our needs, and pursue goals and dreams. Of course, we're expected to be passive at times, and leave certain matters totally in the hands of the Lord. Yet even more frequently, I believe, God expects us to take bold action toward our needs. He deals with us differently at different times—teaching us patience on one occasion, and on another the importance of being proactive, and of taking sometimes scary steps forward. Our discussion ahead should help you better understand when Christ is calling you to the one response, and when the other.

If perchance you've read my *Overcoming Shyness*, you'll find chapter seven on assertiveness borrowed from it, in addition to part of chapter one. The other four chapters are published herefor the first time in book form.

It's my hope that this book will inspire in you both the patience for waiting in faith when it's necessary, and the courage for those vital and frequent times when stepping out in faith is your right course. God's rich blessings as you read!

1

To Wait
or Initiate?

FEW QUESTIONS CONFUSE US MORE as Christians than what it means to live by faith. When does it mean sitting still and leaving a need completely in the hands of Christ? When does it mean taking initiative to solve a problem or reach a goal?

Many serious Christians assume that faith usually means the former and not the latter. Jack longs for a new job that would make better use of his talents. Yet he fears he would be pushing God by going out and looking for one. "Shouldn't I assume that if Christ wants me in a different job, he will bring it along without any effort on my part?" he asks.

Mary Alice, who wants to be married, wrestles with a similar question. She would like to change jobs or even move to a different city where the prospects of meeting someone compatible would be better. Yet she wonders if this would be taking matters too much into her own hands. Doesn't faith demand she do nothing, and wait for Christ to bring the right man directly to her?

Both Jack and Mary Alice would prefer to be doing something specific toward reaching their goals, and they each see clear steps they can take. They both feel frustrated and helpless in the face of dilemmas they feel they can do something to remedy. Yet they fear their efforts would usurp God's authority. Surely faith must require they sit still and wait patiently for him to act.

I remember well carrying this assumption as a young believer, yet I remember too the day when my thinking began to change. I had been considering the possibility of beginning a radio ministry, which seemed a logical outgrowth of my experience in music and my contacts at the time. Yet I felt painfully guilty about doing anything direct to bring this about. I had heard so much talk about being still and waiting on the Lord that it seemed inconceivable he would want me to take any initiative toward this desire.

Finally, I asked an older Christian whom I deeply respected, a member of our church staff, for her counsel. I really expected her to tell me to be passive and wait for the Lord to open any doors. To my surprise, she not only affirmed my dream but recommended I take some determined steps to follow it. Because I thought highly of her and knew she trusted strongly in Christ, I was left feeling much better about taking initiative. Though the radio ministry never got off the ground, her advice helped give me the strength of heart to pursue a music ministry and some other projects in my early years as a believer.

While her counsel helped me over this hump emotionally, I was still uncertain how to resolve the issue biblically, and searched for what Scripture teaches about waiting vs. initiating for some time. I grew intensely interested in how we as believers should seek to understand God's will for our personal choices. This led me to read the Bible cover-to-cover, as slowly and carefully as I could, looking at how individuals in Scripture found God's will. I

Speaking Our Mind

We can expect, too, that this personal initiative will frequently require us to express our convictions clearly with people—even with those who disagree with us—and that God will use this assertiveness to persuade them and open important doors for us. While we must always listen carefully to the counsel others give us and be open to having our insights changed by theirs, we must realize that God will also use us to counsel them and, at times, to correct their misunderstandings. We need to become comfortable with this interactive process. We cannot simply assume that God will always want us to acquiesce if others aren't immediately in favor of our plans. While we need to be considerate and compassionate when asserting ourselves at such times, we shouldn't be reluctant to express our convictions.

We find a wonderfully instructive example of such bold but courteous assertiveness in the biblical account of David interacting with Saul over fighting Goliath. David took the initiative to propose to Saul that he battle the giant. Saul's initial response was negative: "You are not able to go out against this Philistine and fight him; you are only a boy, and he has been a fighting man from his youth" (1 Sam 17:33). Most would have taken this admonition from the most respected warrior in the land not only as wise counsel but as a glorious pardon from responsibility! David now had an easy out. He had done his duty, declared his willingness to go into the heat of battle, but was told he could stay on the sidelines. He could have his cake and eat it too. He could glory in being the only person to volunteer to fight the giant, yet enjoy the freedom of not having to face the challenge.

But David pressed his point with Saul:

Your servant has been keeping his father's sheep. When a lion or a bear came and carried off a sheep from the flock, I went after it, struck it and rescued the sheep from its mouth.

When it turned on me, I seized it by its hair, struck it and killed it. Your servant has killed both the lion and the bear; this uncircumcised Philistine will be like one of them, because he has defied the armies of the living God. The LORD who delivered me from the paw of the lion and the paw of the bear will deliver me from the hand of this Philistine. (1 Sam 17:34-37) Interestingly, Saul wasn't put off by David's straightforwardness. To the contrary, he was changed by it. His response: "Go, and the LORD be with you" (1 Sam 17:37). Even after that, David continued to be respectfully assertive with Saul. He urged that he be allowed to fight Goliath without the cumbersome armor Saul thought he needed, and again Saul conceded. If David had taken the "easy out" and passively accepted Saul's advice, he would have stifled his own development—and in addition, a nation of people would have suffered for his silence. This is, in my impression, the most helpful example we find in Scripture of healthy assertiveness. We see God honoring the efforts of one man to convince an individual considerably more knowledgeable and powerful than himself that he has gifts that should be recognized and put to use. An entire nation benefited from his straightforwardness.

The passage drives home a vital point for each of us. Not only does God bring us to see broader opportunities for investing our lives, but he uses us as agents of change to bring these options about. Walking in faith requires that we assert ourselves. We can find the courage to do this if we believe that God will honor our efforts and that others will benefit from our initiative. David's example gives us rich encouragement at this point.

Pacing Yourself
In taking personal initiative, there are two cautions I would immediately stress. One is that we should consider a step of faith only

if we can pursue it without frenzy, within the time and energy limits the Lord has given us and without jeopardizing other commitments we have already made. The other is that our understanding of which steps of faith to take should grow out of a regular—preferably daily—time alone with Christ, where we carefully think through the direction of our life and what God wants us to do. In general, individuals in Scripture were judged presumptuous not because they took personal initiative, but because they did so without establishing their plans before the Lord (Josh 9:14).

As we daily seek the Lord's direction, we should feel great freedom to take bold initiative to find the best opportunities for using our gifts, building relationships, and pursuing goals and dreams. I remember what great relief I felt as a young Christian when my friend told me it was okay to do this. I hope you'll feel similar relief in realizing the freedom Scripture gives you at this point. The fact is that God gives us greater control to change the circumstances of our lives than we tend to think.

In the chapters that follow, we'll refine this point further. It's enormously liberating to know that we're free—often mandated—to take initiative to solve problems and pursue goals. This puts us in a cherished starting position, as we consider alternatives we have and what specific actions to take. In some cases our path is abundantly clear. There's an obvious step we should take to dig out of a hole we're in, or to move forward with an option that's unquestionably God's best for our life.

In other cases it's less obvious what we should do. We may wonder if we should wait passively for further guidance or take a step of faith with less than perfect certainty about the best course. And so we're thrust back to the wait-or-initiate question again.

On these less-than-certain occasions, certain inclinations serve us well, and position us to act wisely. They help define the proactive spirit that best enables us to live our Christian life wholeheartedly and effectively. These inclinations are what we'll focus on in the chapters ahead, and they include—

• *A bent toward assuming good solutions will come, and a commitment to continue looking for them.* When we're faced with a personal need or problem that seems without solution, or a dream we're uncertain how to pursue, it's easy to let our minds get lazy and to give up looking for an answer. We may even assume the most reverent response is just to wait passively for God to bring an answer, and not to take it on ourselves to look for one. Yet it's important to understand how God has fashioned our minds, and how our problem-solving process works. He has given us the ability to find good solutions, and with time they often come, sometimes suddenly. But we have to continue striving for them. And we most honor Christ by making this effort, for we're taking responsibility, and exercising the problem-solving talent he has put within us. We'll look at this dynamic in chapter two, "The Eureka Factor," and the importance of staying committed to finding solutions when we're confused about what to do.

• *A bent toward acting, even when "all the facts are not in."* At the same time, we can be too perfectionist about the options we'll choose, and especially about the steps toward reaching a long-term goal or dream. There are many occasions when, in the name of keeping our life in motion, we need to choose an alternative that seems less-than-perfect yet is the best option available at the time. It's through this momentum that we best position ourselves for happy surprises and God's fullest provision for our needs. We'll explore this factor in chapter three, "Keeping Your Life in Motion."

• *A bent toward long-range thinking and toward pursuing the goals and dreams God most clearly inspires in us.* As crucial as staying in motion is, we can be tempted to jump at an opportunity simply because it's available, when, with patience and careful strategy, we can find one that better suits the gifts and aspirations God has given us. Yet turning away from the immediate option can be hard, for we wonder if God is beckoning us through such a wide open door. We'll consider this issue in chapter four, "Golden Opportunities and God's Will."

• *A bent toward persisting ("importunity") when praying for specific help from God.* We face the wait-or-initiate question not only with actions we can take, but with our prayer life as well. And especially with "prayers of petition," that is those that make specific requests of God. We may wonder how appropriate it is to persist with a request when no answer has come after a reasonable time. Is it more reverent to simply express our need carefully to God, then leave it in his hands with no further mention? Or are we responsible to continue praying until we receive a clear response? This will be our concern in chapter five, "Am I Praying in God's Will or Against It?"

• *A bent toward asserting ourselves when others treat us unfairly.* We've noted the importance of asserting ourselves when we need others' help. We face the question also, of whether to speak our mind or hold our peace, when others treat us unfairly, hurt us or let us down. We may assume the most loving and Christ-honoring response is to stay silent, and to leave the matter in God's hands. But unless we have reason to think strategic silence will be effective, we're responsible to express our concerns calmly but clearly to those who offend us. While this responsibility means a certain burden, it's reassuring to understand the liberty and calling we have to be assertive on these occasions. We'll look at this topic in chapter six, "Faith and Assertiveness."

Our overriding point in this book is that we're called to take initiative as Christians when we have the chance to do something constructive, to solve a problem or to move our life forward in some significant way. This initiative may include action, prayer, and asserting ourselves with others. As a rule, we should be strongly bent toward *doing something*, even when the options before us seem less than perfect. Yet when we've established a goal or dream, and have reason to believe it's God-inspired, we should be cautious about choosing options that divert us from our long-term purpose, even when a door seems unusually wide open.

Few topics in the Christian life are more encouraging and stimulating to consider than the one we're exploring here. I hope our discussion inspires you to take your gifts and aspirations more seriously, and frees you to realize your potential more fully for Christ!

2

The Eureka Factor

A YOUNG MAN WHO WORKS for our lawn service came by to rake our leaves. As he was getting ready to leave after finishing, I asked him if he would also clean our gutters. I reminded him that his supervisor had assured me this would be done. Because our home is surrounded by oak trees and it was late fall, our gutter problem was serious.

"I'm not able to do it today," he replied, "because I don't have a ladder in my truck. I'll need to come back next week when I can bring one with me."

Once I understood his predicament, I realized that of course he couldn't possibly work on our roof that day. Though disappointed, I told him, "I understand; just do it when you can come back with a ladder."

Only after he left did it dawn on me that I have several large ladders quite adequate to scale the roof of our one-story home.

Why didn't I think to suggest he use one of them?

Lazy thinking is the answer. It's well recognized in psychology (and in sales and marketing strategy) that when someone offers us a *reason* why something can't be done, we default toward accepting it. An explanation persuades us, so often, not by its logic but because its effect is hypnotic. We take it mindlessly as the final word, and don't bother to think beyond it. My failure to see an obvious answer to a simple problem that autumn morning is a textbook example of how this can happen.

This "explanation effect" is merely one of many reasons we may fail to see a situation realistically. We assume we're thinking clearly, yet miss a critical detail that makes all the difference. Our minds can be *very* lazy. We each have many blind spots, and our capacity for skewed perception is far greater than we usually imagine. At times we fail to see the hippopotamus in the wading pool in front of us; the answer to a major problem is staring us in the face, yet we miss it.

The other side of this story is equally interesting. When we are able to move beyond our blind spots and cloudy thinking, and open our minds creatively to solving problems, we are often able to see solutions that have eluded us. The answers that come are sometimes downright surprising.

Some years ago, our family was living in a townhouse and my office was in the basement. Because an open stairway connected the basement and the first floor, I was often distracted by noise from upstairs. The obvious solution would be to install a door. Yet since the stairway had an open, expansive design, I couldn't think of any logical way to fit a door into the wide space at the top or bottom of the stairs. I spent considerable time mulling the problem over, trying to come up with a workable design. I concluded there was no solution short of a major modification to the stairway, which would violate the community's architectural standards and be too expensive to undertake.

One evening, though, I shared my dilemma at a Bible study. A member whom I respected for his problem-solving skills responded that he was sure there was an easy answer. His confidence inspired me, and I thought, *He's right, there must be a way to do it.* The next day it dawned on me that I could insert a door at the landing point where the stairway turned halfway down; since the stairwell was more enclosed there, this modification was easy to make. The solution was, in fact, so obvious and simple that I couldn't believe I hadn't thought of it before.

Finding Answers to Impossible Problems

Each of us enjoys such breakthrough moments of insight from time to time, when the answer to a perplexing problem suddenly becomes clear. Few experiences are more thrilling—especially when we've grown convinced a problem is unsolvable. We feel like dropping everything and celebrating. We understand how Archimedes, who discovered the principle of buoyancy while bathing, could have sprung from his tub and run unadorned through the streets of Syracuse, crying, "Eureka" ("I've found it") (though hopefully we're not inspired to repeat his feat).

We have a continual need for such epiphanies as we move through life. Life presents us with an ongoing array of problems to solve and decisions to make. They range from less than earth-shattering *(How can I fix this flat tire without a jack? What topic should I choose for this term paper? How can I stop this leak in my kitchen? Who can I ask to the dance?)*, to much more monumental *(How can I find work in this field when no one's hiring? How can I gain admission to this grad program with a GPI of 2.5? Where can I find help for this knee pain that's killing me? How can I find someone to marry?)*.

Invariably, we each encounter certain problems that seem to

defy solution. Though we long to find an answer to them, we grow convinced there is none. At this point the tragedy is that we may close ourselves off to finding a solution. Even worse, we may use our powers of intellect from then on to convince ourselves of all the reasons the problem cannot be solved—and so the more we ponder it, the more intractable it seems.

Yet answers often can be found to life's "impossible" problems, when we open our minds and hearts fully to discovering them. Here it helps us immensely to appreciate two factors that we easily overlook: One is the problem-solving nature of the mind God has placed within us; the other is the help God extends to us in resolving problems and decisions when we ask for it. Let's look at both of these extraordinary life benefits.

Our Mind's Creative Nature
First, the mind. It's the nature of the mind God has given us to seek and find good solutions to the problems we face. To say it more strongly, he has hard-wired our brains to do so. We're beginning from a much greater position of strength than we usually realize.

The Gestalt psychologists of the 1920's and 30's were the first in the history of psychology to appreciate this fact. Psychology at the time was dominated by behaviorism, with its mechanistic view of human thinking. Humans are simply a higher form of animal, behaviorists held, who solve problems through a tedious process of trial and error. The Gestaltists took a deeper look and saw something more profound. When we face a problem, they observed, our mind instinctively seeks to bring to it a "gestalt"—which is German for form or shape. And in àn instant, we may make a giant leap forward, moving beyond trial and error to a good solution.

Even animals from the more intelligent species are capable of such gestalts, these researchers showed. In one experiment, Wolfgang Köhler placed Sultan, a hungry male chimpanzee, in a room with a bunch of bananas hanging from the ceiling. Sultan first made several attempts to leap at them, finding them well out of reach. Then he discovered a stick and a box well-removed from the bananas. Sultan grabbed the stick and attempted to strike the bananas, but again they were too high. He bounced around the cage, angry and frustrated. Then suddenly he stopped, went to the box and shoved it under the bananas. He climbed on it and, with a small leap, knocked the bananas down with his stick.

After futilely attempting to solve his problem through random trial and error, Sultan's mind suddenly fast-forwarded to the right solution. Köhler saw in this episode, and many like it in experiments with primates, a parallel to how the human mind works in solving much more complicated problems. We begin by trying one possibility, then another, exhausting our options step by step, yet only hitting roadblocks. Then our brain suddenly functions on a deeper level, producing an answer so remarkably appropriate that we wonder how it had escaped us until now.

Our Subconscious Ally

Köhler and his associates[1] were more concerned with demonstrating the fact that our mind functions this way than with explaining how it happens. Psychologists after them, though, came increasingly to appreciate the role that our subconscious plays in this process. It's now widely understood that much of our thinking takes place subconsciously. And our subconscious mind typically does a much better job at creative thinking than our conscious mind. We may feel we're making no progress in solving a difficult problem, when in fact our subconscious is wrestling with it earnestly. In time, a welcome solution may suddenly emerge consciously, with all the impact of a divine revelation.

Poet Amy Lowell describes such an experience in composing a poem:

How carefully and precisely the subconscious mind functions, I have often been a witness to in my own work. An idea will come into my head for no apparent reason; "The Bronze Horses," for instance. I registered the horses as a good subject for a poem; and, having so registered them, I consciously thought no more about the matter. But what I had really done was to drop my subject into the subconscious, much as one drops a letter into the mail-box. Six months later, the words of the poem began to come into my head; the poem—to use my private vocabulary—was "there."[2]

Countless writers, artists, composers and scientific thinkers attest to episodes similar to Lowell's, of sudden inspiration in their own work—often following an unproductive period. Their experiences document the uncanny way the subconscious mind works, and help explain how creative thinking occurs. We're reminded that much more mental activity is going on beneath the surface in our heads than we tend to think. And we're helped to understand an important aspect of how God has fashioned human life.

Our Continual Need for God's Help
However the creative process is understood, the Gestaltists were the first to appreciate its implications—especially for solving the normal problems of life. What they saw, plainly and simply, is that our mind inclines toward finding good solutions to our challenges.

This basic insight is an extremely redemptive one for us as Christians. It helps us appreciate a vital feature of the mind God has placed within us, and an important part of what it means to be made in the image of God. God has given us the ability to think constructively, and to find answers even to some of our most vexing problems.

This doesn't mean that he has created us to function effectively without his help. We desperately need his Lordship and his constant influence in our life. Apart from his help, we sabotage our own interests in countless ways, and our mind may form gestalts that reflect anything but his best for our life.

But when God provides for us in any area, he normally does so by influencing the natural processes of life that he has created rather than by overriding them. This means that when he guides us, he typically does so, not by giving us a direct revelation, but by guiding the mind he has given us, enabling it to function as he intended. Appreciating this process deepens our sense of purpose, for we recognize that God has given us a role in solving the predicaments we face.

Yet it also reminds us that we are dependent on God for life and breath and the ability to think clearly. The point never comes in our lives when we no longer need God's help in resolving problems, and now are able to run on automatic pilot. The good news is that when we ask God for wisdom, Scripture promises he *will* provide it (Jas 1:5). We may be confident that the God who has given us our mind will help it reach wise conclusions when we humbly ask for his assistance.

The concept of gestalt increases our confidence that this wisdom will come when we pray for it, for we realize that even if we're at an impasse, a moment of insight may suddenly break through that makes all the difference. Any day may bring with it the enlightenment we need to move forward. We have strong reason for hope.

Gestalts in Scripture

To this end, Scripture provides us with many examples of individuals who found answers to the most challenging personal problems, often when they had practically lost hope. We see people enjoying relief and the chance to make new beginnings, from experiences of gestalt that surely surprised them in many cases. Their examples encourage us to be patient and hopeful that we'll find the insight we need to turn around difficult circumstances in our own life. Some of the most inspiring examples include:

• *The prodigal son (Lk 15:11-31).* This young man left his supportive home, moved to a distant country, and through wild living and many bad judgments squandered his inheritance. A famine then set in. Things grew so bleak for him that he "hired himself out to a citizen of that country, who sent him to his fields to feed pigs. He longed to fill his stomach with the pods that the pigs were eating, but no one gave him anything." He clearly felt he had no alternative but to live a pitiful, poverty-stricken existence.

Finally, though, he "came to his senses." It occurred to him that his father's servants enjoyed far better living conditions than his, and they had plenty to eat. He would go back home, apologize profusely to his father, and ask for the privilege of serving as one of his hired hands. Of course, when he followed through and returned home, his father welcomed him exuberantly and hosted a great celebration for his return. Every indication is that he was restored to his full status as a son in the family. At the point when things seemed most hopeless, one moment of gestalt brought a solution, and a vast improvement to his life.

• *The woman with the hemorrhage (Mk 5:24-34).* Equally destitute, but through no fault of her own, was a woman the Gospels describe as having suffered a blood flow for twelve years. She had exhausted her finances seeking medical help, yet her condition only continued to deteriorate. Then came an unexpected opportunity to encounter Jesus—and with it a gestalt: "If I just touch his clothes, I will be healed." That insight proved to be life-changing in the most thoroughgoing sense. After pushing through a crowd and touching his robe, she experienced healing, then received a profound compliment from Jesus about her faith.

• *Paul's decision to visit Macedonia (Acts 16:6-10)*. During a particularly difficult period in his ministry, Paul and his missionary team experienced several substantial setbacks. They were thwarted in major attempts to enter both Asia and Bithynia. Then they ended up in Troas, but apparently didn't feel conditions were right for ministry there. One night, though, Paul had a dream of a man in Macedonia begging for his help. In the morning, after Paul described his dream to his friends, they quickly arrived at a gestalt: God was calling them to evangelize Macedonia. In a moment, they moved from confusion about their mission to a clear direction: "we got ready at once to leave for Macedonia."

Their visit to Macedonia (Acts 16:11-40), while not without challenges (which went with the territory in Paul's ministry), resulted in many conversions and the establishing of a church. Paul's central mission of breaking ground for the gospel in unevangelized territory was accomplished.

• *Isaiah in the temple (Is 6)*. Isaiah, distraught over King Uzziah's death and over the moral and spiritual decay in his nation, enters the temple. During a brief time of worship he experiences a startling paradigm shift: God is looking for someone not just to lament Israel's problems, but to address and remedy them. "Then I heard the voice of the Lord saying, 'Whom shall I send? And who will go for us?'"

Isaiah's exuberant reply: "Here am I. Send me!"

• *Abraham's search for a wife for Isaac (Gen 24)*. When Genesis describes Abraham's decision to send his servant to Haran to seek a wife for his son Isaac, it begins by noting: "Abraham was now old and well advanced in years, and the LORD had blessed him in every way." Why does the writer start with this detail?

It is probably right to say that while God had blessed Abraham beyond measure, considerable time had passed and Isaac was still unmarried. It's likely Abraham had tried earnestly to find Isaac a spouse in Canaan, only to discover that his son wasn't compatible with the women there. Abraham had probably been confused for some time about how to help Isaac find a mate. If so, then the idea of going to Haran must have come as a remarkable epiphany. Abraham realized he wasn't bound by geography in seeking Isaac a wife, but could go elsewhere—in this case, to his home region. That insight—that gestalt—came with strong conviction, and the confidence that God would send his angel ahead and give success to the mission.

The servant's venture to Haran, of course, was victorious. He returned with Rebecca, who became Isaac's wife, and the rest is history.

• *Jacob's decision to leave Laban and return to his home (Gen 31).* Jacob worked for many years as a shepherd for his uncle Laban in Haran. Laban treated Jacob increasingly unfairly as time wore on, and the situation grew more and more frustrating for Jacob and his ever-growing family. Yet Jacob still felt loyal to Laban and compelled to stay.

That is, until what was undoubtedly a stunning moment of revelation. "Then the LORD said to Jacob, 'Go back to the land of your fathers and to your relatives, and I will be with you.'"

It's very likely that Jacob had wanted to return home for some time, and so God was confirming that what Jacob wanted to do was appropriate. God was giving him permission to leave his intolerable circumstances.

This example is helpful for any of us who is in a demoralizing situation that we feel guilty about leaving. It reminds us that God may be giving us permission—even a mandate—to move on. The realization that God wants us to leave an abusive situation can be a true Eureka moment—as it surely was for Jacob.

Two Ways God Guides Us

Jacob's epiphany that he should leave Haran is interesting from another angle, for we're told that God spoke directly to him about what to do. It's not clear that God did so in any of the other examples just cited.[3] Scripture cites numerous cases where God gave someone supernatural direction, as he did here with Jacob. Yet for any individual in Scripture—even Biblical heroes—such guidance was the exception, usually the rare exception to that person's normal experience. Genesis notes only several instances when God intervened in Jacob's life with a direct revelation, for instance.

Still, these examples are important, for they remind us that God will find a way to give us the insight we need. In most cases he will do so by influencing our mind to function naturally and effectively, so that we reach an inspired solution through our normal mental process. Yet on a special occasion, when our need requires, he may break the rules of nature and communicate to us directly—either through some dramatic means, or by enabling us to come quickly to a conclusion we never could have reached through reason alone.

Appreciating this fact is unspeakably encouraging, for it deepens our confidence that God cares enough to guide us, and will give us exactly the guidance we need, when we need it. He has two means to do so—through influencing our normal thought process, or by bypassing it and communicating with us directly.

In some cases it's impossible to know whether God has guided us directly or not. Those wonderful moments of gestalt that we enjoy from time to time, when we suddenly recognize a solution to a problem that's long puzzled us, often feel as though we're experiencing a supernatural revelation from God. Yet whether in fact we are, or whether an insight from our subconscious mind has simply bubbled to the surface, may be impossible to determine. And we usually don't need to know which way it happened. The important thing is that God has guided us, whether directly, or by influencing our thinking; in either case, he has found a way to give us the enlightenment we need.

What the biblical examples we've just looked at, and many others like them, show us most importantly, is that good solutions to problems tend to come when we stay open, hopeful, and inquisitive about finding them. And sometimes they emerge as a sudden epiphany—a stunning answer to a problem we thought beyond hope. The Gestalt psychologists, while not working under any religious or spiritual convictions, stumbled upon an insight into how God has created us that's immensely helpful to understand, and helps us appreciate what it means to be created in his image.

Thus, when Scripture first declares that we're made in God's image, it's at the beginning of the Bible, just after the description of God's creating the universe, earth, vegetation and animal life. "Then God said, 'Let us make man in our image, in our likeness, and let them rule over the fish of the sea and the birds of the air, over the livestock, over all the earth, and over all the creatures that move along the ground'" (Gen 1:26). The placement of this extraordinary statement just after the creation narrative is surely not accidental, but meant to say that we're made in the image of One who *creates*. To be in God's image means being endowed with the ability to think and act creatively, and to find redemptive answers to the needs we and others experience. That we're endowed with practical problem-solving skills is shown also in our calling announced in this verse—to have dominion over the earth. Honoring God, then, means using this ability to the best ends we can, trusting that as we strive to be productive, God will influence our mind to good solutions.

Opening Our Mind and Heart to Good Solutions

And so we come to another fascinating angle on the wait-or-initiate question that's our concern in this book. When we need a solution to a problem or need we're facing, or a strategy for reaching a goal, it makes huge sense to continue actively looking for it. God has endowed us with problem-solving ability, which he guides as we use it prayerfully and responsibly, and with the right time and effort a welcome answer so often comes. Of course, this also means waiting patiently in faith for the solution to emerge—but waiting hopefully, expectantly, and as actively as possible. A burden, then, is laid on us from both directions. But, especially, the responsibility is on us to keeping striving for good solutions, to persist till they come, and to understand this effort as an important part of obedience to Christ.

We need, in short, a proactive spirit toward solving the problems and needs that come across our path, and an optimistic conviction that they *can* be solved. Here, though, a caution needs to be sounded. Our problem-solving zeal needs to be tempered with a realistic understanding that the step we need to take on a given occasion may be difficult, or may seem less-than-ideal from our standpoint. Here, the attitude that serves us best is one committed to staying in motion as much as possible, and which appreciates that stepping out in faith generally is more Christ-honoring than waiting in faith, when we have the opportunity to do something at least potentially productive toward our need. We'll look more closely at this principle in the next chapter.

3

Keeping Your
Life in Motion

DURING MOST OF HIS ADULT LIFE, Emmett Kirkland worked for Watkins Realty. Emmett, my wife, Evie's grandfather, was a master craftsman, who maintained rental properties for the Pittsburgh firm.

As the Great Depression set in, the company's rental income dried up, and Mr. Watkins laid off Emmett. Like countless others, Emmett fell victim to the economic fallout of the times. Like few others, he countered his setback with an unusual response. He informed Mr. Watkins that if the company was unable to salary him, he would continue serving it—*for free*. He reasoned it was better to stay active and productive, than to sit idly at home bemoaning his lot.

Emmett's decision to continue working without pay proved fortunate in many ways. His positive spirit inspired his wife and five children to be resourceful, and to find creative solutions to the family's needs. His dedicated service to Watkins Realty helped it continue to meet clients' needs and to weather its financial crisis. On occasion, when revenue was more than anticipated, Mr. Watkins shared some of the windfall with Emmett. And when the company's hard times finally eased, Emmett, of course, was the first to be rehired.

Although I was never privileged to meet him, Emmett Kirkland is on the short list of my personal heroes, for I've seen his influence upon his son Glenn—Evie's father—and, through Glenn, upon her. What's most impressive about Emmett's response to the layoff is that he took action when the natural response would have been inaction. This magnanimous step of faith brought great benefits to him, his family and numerous others.

Small Steps That Make a Major Difference
We each experience a multitude of setbacks and losses during our own lifetime. So often our instinctive response to them is immobility. We're stunned by the disappointment, and unable to think clearly about what to do.

It's easy enough to get moving again when there is some *radical* new beginning we can make—a major change, so grandiose that it fuels our energy and hope. It's typical, too, when we're depressed, to imagine that only a major improvement will solve our problems. We look with contempt upon the small and routine steps we can take to improve our life. Yet often these are precisely what will break the spell of our depression and open us to God's fresh provision for our needs.

My own grandfather, Milton Smith, suffered an extraordinary loss as a young man, when his wife of ten years died. They were both only in their later twenties at the time.

Several years later, while working as a traffic patrolman in Washington, D.C., he stopped a car for exceeding the (yes) eighteen-miles-an-hour speed limit around Dupont Circle. The chance encounter led to a friendship with the driver, Katherine Horton, then a romance, then—marriage. One remarkable moment brought a cherished relationship that forever changed his life and healed the grief of losing his first love. Yet God's provision came through the most routine of activities for him—a traffic stop.

Undoubtedly, my granddad began that day expecting nothing unusual. Perhaps he didn't want to go to work at all. Yet he went, plodding ahead with his routine responsibilities. His experience reminds us how simply keeping our life in motion sometimes opens us suddenly to help from God that we dearly welcome.

A New Beginning for Moses
We learn this lesson from an incident in Moses' early life. When he was about forty years old, he killed an Egyptian whom he caught beating an Israelite. Moses thought he was acting heroically. Yet he soon found that Pharaoh wanted to kill him for his vigilantism; his fellow Jews were also angry at him, for stirring up trouble for them with the Egyptians.

Moses then fled from Egypt to the neighboring Midian (Ex 2:11-25). There, "he sat down by a well." It is hard to imagine anyone feeling more isolated and helpless than Moses must have at this moment. He had abandoned the privileged environment of Pharaoh's palace, his friends and everything familiar, and now was alone and destitute in a strange land. He may have thought that he had no options for rebuilding his life.

But soon an opportunity arose to do something constructive. The daughters of the priest of Midian "came and drew water, and filled the troughs to water their father's flock." Shepherds came and chased the women and their sheep away. Moses then assisted these frightened women, brought them back to the well, protected them from the shepherds, and helped them water their flock.

From what we know of Moses' assertive personality and physical strength, this act of chivalry must have seemed second nature to him—simply the obvious response at that moment. Yet the women reported Moses' deed to their father, Jethro, who was greatly impressed. Jethro befriended Moses, then provided him a home, a job tending his sheep, and a wife—his daughter Zipporah.

One act of kindness on Moses' part opened the door to his finding a new family, enjoyable employment, a marriage partner and a comfortable living situation for the next forty years. By merely rising to the occasion and doing what was natural, Moses took a step that brought God's extravagant provision for his needs.

Finding God's Best by Doing the Obvious
What emerges from Moses' experience is one of the most helpful principles of guidance presented in Scripture. To say it simply: we find much of God's will for our life by doing the obvious.

Because God's providence is operating fully in our lives when we follow Christ, he conveys much of his guidance through the normal responsibilities and opportunities of everyday life, including many routine activities. Martin Luther spoke of God's preaching a "daily sermon" to us through these circumstances. He meant that God gives us *guidance* through them, as clear and vital as if he were speaking to us in an audible voice.

The most encouraging part is that by merely doing the ordinary, we occasionally put ourselves in position to enjoy an unusual blessing from God—the type we might imagine could result only from taking a major, carefully-planned step of faith. We should remember Moses' experience in Midian often, especially when we've suffered a defeat and can't see any way to make a fresh start.

The Benefits of Keeping Our Life in Motion
Appreciating how God guides us through the circumstances of

daily life can do wonders to revive our hope, not only when we experience setbacks, but when the pattern of our day-to-day life becomes too repetitive or boring. We can be confident there is purpose in our plodding ahead, for as we're faithful to our responsibilities, God is full of surprises.

Keeping our life in motion is critical when it comes to reaching goals. We're better able to think creatively when we're actively pursuing a goal, than when we're merely considering doing so. As we overcome inertia and move forward, our subconscious rallies and helps us solve problems that otherwise elude us. Just getting started on a project is often half the battle. Vincent van Gogh advised aspiring artists:

> One must not work in a thousand fears, and yet that is what many do who are so anxious to get hold of the right colors and tones that through this very anxiety they become like tepid water. The real artists say, "Just dash the color on!" Otherwise, we reach the summit of wisdom when nobody has any daring left.

Van Gogh's advice applies to each of us, in any endeavor we undertake. We can spend too much time analyzing our options, and wait too long to get started. Sometimes we do better just to "dash the color on." As we begin moving toward our goal, we're better able to recognize how to reach it.

We also make it easier for others to help us when we're taking clear steps toward a goal, for they are better able to recognize specific ways to assist us. Their incentive to help us is greater, too, when they see that we're serious.

In addition, we present a better role model to others when we're being productive and not merely sitting still. When Emmett Kirkland chose to work unsalaried for Watkins Realty, he made a lasting impression on his children about the value of work, the importance of faithfulness, and the benefits of staying hopeful.

His behavior did more to demonstrate to them what trusting Christ involves than any words could ever have conveyed. His legacy inspired them to be optimistic, to work hard, to tackle problems rather than run away from them, and to vigorously trust the Lord to meet their needs.

We each have far greater influence on other people than we imagine. And we do leave a legacy. When we approach life positively, we inspire others to do the same.

Beyond Futility

How easily we fall into futility. The effort to improve our life just isn't worth it, we assume, and the prospects of success are too remote to merit pursuing a dream.

Appreciating how fully God is at work in the circumstances of our daily life can give us the heart to press on. It *is* wonderful when, from time to time, we are able to take major, triumphant steps of faith. Yet in between such occasions, we can enjoy the same exhilaration of faith in taking the more mundane steps, knowing we're participating in God's bigger picture for our life.

And sometimes, even the most routine step opens us to an unexpected blessing from God. This is a basis for beginning each day with the highest expectations, and for living it with energy and hope. And we do well to begin each day remembering that, generally, we better honor God by staying in motion than by sitting still.

There is an exception, though, and an important one. We're responsible before Christ to understand the gifts and motivational pattern he has placed within us—in short, to have a good grasp of our individuality. In light of this insight, we need to establish goals and dreams that enable us to best realize our potential. And pursuing an important goal requires that we avoid diversions. The challenge can come when we have the chance to do something productive—perhaps something we would otherwise welcome doing—that would divert us from our long-term purpose. If the door for this opportunity is wide open, it can be especially confusing to know what God is beckoning us to do. We'll look at this interesting challenge in the next chapter.

4

Golden Opportunities and God's Will

HERE'S A PROBLEM YOU MIGHT SAY is nice to have.

You have an opportunity. A golden opportunity. The chance to develop a serious relationship, or to marry. Or a job opening with generous pay and benefits. Or an invitation from your pastor to direct one of your church's important ministries.

At first you're euphoric, stunned at your good fortune, flattered that someone believes in you so strongly.

Then, with time and reflection, come the reality checks: The relationship is too high maintenance. The job doesn't fit you well. The church position doesn't match your spiritual gifts.

Still, the door is so *wide* open. How could you possibly turn your back on such a wonderful prospect?

We each face this dilemma from time to time. And while we welcome the problem on one level (it's nice simply to have an open door), the agony of deciding can be extreme. The problem is great enough for anyone, regardless of their spiritual outlook. For the Christian, though, questions about God's will can add to the confusion. "If Christ is in control of my life, shouldn't I assume that a shining opportunity like this is from him? Isn't he showing his intention through this open door? Aren't I sinning if I turn away from it?"

Some of our most confusing struggles about God's guidance concern the meaning of open doors. We wonder if respect for God's providence ("God opened the door, so I must go through it") should override stewardship of our life and common sense ("the opportunity doesn't work for me, so I shouldn't pursue it").

Different Responses to Open Doors

There's no question that God uses circumstances to guide us. Paul placed important weight upon open doors in determining which regions God wanted him to visit during his missionary travels. "I will stay in Ephesus until Pentecost," he writes, "for a wide door for effective work has opened to me" (1 Cor 16:8-9 RSV). Paul says nothing here about God's giving him direct guidance to stay in Ephesus, but merely notes that the situation is ideal for him to minister. This example isn't isolated. Paul based many a decision to stay in a certain area and evangelize on the fact that a prime opportunity for ministry was present.

Yet Paul turned away from good opportunities as well. "When I came to Troas to preach the gospel of Christ," he also writes, "a door was opened for me in the Lord; but my mind could not rest because I did not find my brother Titus there. So I took leave of them and went on to Macedonia" (2 Cor 2:12-13 RSV). Paul clearly perceived that God had opened this door for him in Troas, yet he also concluded that God didn't want him to go through it! His example shows graphically that God may provide us with an opportunity which he doesn't wish us to accept. And this may be true even though we recognize that God himself has opened a particular door.

Jesus, like Paul, also responded to circumstances unpredictably. In general, he took open doors seriously. He healed every individual noted in Scripture who asked for his help. And when it came to selecting his twelve disciples, he didn't launch a worldwide search for the perfect dozen, but picked from those available in the small sector of the world where he had chosen to minister.

Yet he decided not to respond to certain beckoning opportunities as well. Once, when he was visiting Capernaum, his disciples reported to him, "Everyone is looking for you" (Mk 1:37 Phillips). They informed him that the situation in Capernaum was ripe for his ministry—that many were eager for his teaching and healing.

Jesus' response? "Then we will go somewhere else, to the neighboring towns, so that I may give my message there too—that is why I have come" (Mk 1:38 Phillips).

What's fascinating in this case is that the presence of a great opportunity to teach and heal helped Jesus resolve to go somewhere else! A significant opening for ministry in Capernaum helped him reaffirm his priority—that he was called to minister not just in one setting, but in a variety of them, during his brief earthly mission.

Not Jumping to Conclusions
The fact that both Jesus and Paul sometimes walked away from prime opportunities, after weighing them carefully, highlights a benefit of the open door that we seldom consider. When an opportunity to take a significant step with our life is actually present, we're able to interact with it, intellectually and emotionally, on a

level not possible when we're merely musing about it as a distant possibility. Having a real-life option to grapple with breaks us out of the realm of fantasy and focuses our thinking remarkably. We are able to gaze down the road, and grasp more realistically what it would be like to truly live out this role.

Even if we conclude that the opportunity isn't right for us, we have still benefited greatly from its being present. This explains why God might open a door for us—even a wide one—yet not expect us to venture through it, as paradoxical as that may sound. This aspect of God's guidance is immensely liberating, for it means we're not obligated to any assumption about his will when a compelling option presents itself, but are free—indeed, expected—to weigh it along with other factors. While God gives us guidance through every open door we encounter, he means for us to accept the opportunity in one case, but to learn from it and turn away from it in another.

A friend of mine, Victor, entered college intent on becoming a physician. His father, a prominent surgeon, had long encouraged him to pursue a medical career. As a college senior, Victor applied to various med schools and, due partly to his father's influence, was admitted to the one he most wished to attend.

Acceptance by *any* medical college is a cherished accomplishment for a premed student. And admission to your *top* choice is an extraordinary triumph. Add to this the family pressure, and Victor had strong reasons to stay the course toward his longtime goal of becoming a doctor.

During his junior year of college, though, Victor had given his life to Christ. He became active in a campus ministry and in a local church as well. By the time he was ready to graduate, he had discovered he had significant gifts for ministry and a strong motivation to become a pastor. He found the courage to turn down the prestigious med school's offer in favor of going to seminary.

Though it was difficult to decline such a tantalizing prospect, the fact that it was available helped him resolve firmly that his self-understanding had changed, and that God had placed a new aspiration in his heart to which he must be faithful.

His is a good example to keep in mind, for we need all the reinforcement we can get in striving to think clearly about open doors. We easily default to thinking God wants us to proceed through them. It can be excruciating to decline a great opportunity, and the decision can be complicated further by our view of God's guidance. Yet even the best prospect may be God's means of educating us and sharpening our vision for taking a different direction.

Remarkable Coincidences

If it's natural to think that God is giving us a clear message through golden opportunities to go forward, it's even more tempting to think so when circumstances are highly coincidental. I know of a man and woman who met each other while each was traveling separately in Europe. They enjoyed some time together, but returned to the United States not expecting to meet again. Later, they encountered each other unexpectedly in a large metropolitan church. They took this unlikely occurrence as God's sign they should marry.

Tragically, the marriage lasted only six months. Theirs was a classic case of reading too much guidance into a coincidence. It was an exceptional coincidence, to be sure. They would have been justified in concluding that God was showing them *something* through this unusual occurrence—perhaps that they should get better acquainted. But they jumped to conclusions about his ultimate intention for their relationship, without doing the hard work of getting to know each other well.

Over the course of a lifetime—and by the law of averages—

each of us will experience certain turns of event so unusual and coincidental that it appears for all the world that God is giving us special guidance through them. We should be extremely cautious of our conclusions at such times. God may be using a coincidence to get our attention in some way. But we should stay tentative about *what* he is prompting us to do until we've looked at all the related factors. Sometimes the conclusion we reach, after a deep breath and many second thoughts, defies our first assumption.

Confidence in Providence

While we can be too quick to jump to conclusions about God's will when circumstances are favorable or coincidental, we can also be too slow to recognize when opportunities truly are right for us. This is the other challenge we face in weighing the significance of open doors. We need to be properly cautious in considering them; yet we also need to learn to see them with the eyes of faith. God provides us with many opportunities that are well suited for us, and that are his means of moving us forward. Yet, as we noted in the last chapter, these opportunities sometimes fall short of certain ideals or expectations we have, and so we may fail to perceive them as God's best alternatives.

One problem in this case is that fantasy is always more enticing than reality. God provides us with *real-life options*, which he sees as ideal for us. Yet the fact that they're *available* may keep us from appreciating them as fully as we should.

In his missionary travels, Paul often settled for opportunities to minister that fell short of his expectations. Such was his experience in Macedonia. A man appeared to him in a dream one night, pleading, "Come over to Macedonia and help us" (Acts 16:9). In the morning, Paul and his companions concluded God was calling them to travel there. They ventured forth to that city, surely expecting to find the man of Paul's dream active in ministry there.

Instead, they found a Jewish woman, Lydia, leading a women's prayer group by a river. Paul spent some time with these women, and through his influence Lydia committed her life to Christ. She then persuaded Paul and his team to lodge at her home, where a church soon blossomed (Acts 16:13-15, 40).

Paul had come to Macedonia in response to a vision he had experienced—of a man active in ministry begging for his help. Yet to accommodate himself to the reality he found once in Macedonia, Paul was willing to modify his vision in two important ways: He accepted that the person he was to assist was a woman, not a man. And she wasn't active in Christian ministry when Paul arrived, but had to be converted first!

Weighing Open Doors in Light of Our Priorities

Paul was able to adjust his expectations and to act decisively in this case *because* he had a keen sense of his priorities. His chief goal was to present the gospel in regions unfamiliar with Christ— a role that fit Paul's gifts and motivational pattern extremely well. In light of this overriding intention, Paul simply looked for open doors. His confidence in God's providence was so strong that he assumed a suitable opportunity to evangelize new territory was God's will for him, unless proven otherwise. The chance to work with Lydia and her friends to launch a church in Macedonia was a good opportunity—and so even though it meant revising his initial assumptions about how he would evangelize this country, he chose to proceed.

On the other hand, Paul felt equal freedom to turn down a good opportunity to minister, if it didn't fit his priorities well or presented significant obstacles to his being an effective icebreaker for the gospel. He chose to walk away from an open door in

Troas, as we've seen, because a key associate—Titus—wasn't present to assist him.

The most important lesson about guidance and circumstances that we learn from Paul's experience is that we should evaluate open doors in light of clear priorities. We need, first and foremost, to come to grips with which of our gifts, talents and desires are the most significant and the ones that God most wants us to emphasize. We should keep this self-understanding in the forefront of our mind as we consider committing to various opportunities.

We should operate also with strong confidence in God's providence—believing as a matter of faith that he will provide us with significant opportunities which allow us to realize our potential. We should carry a bias—that an option which matches our potential and interests reasonably well, and has had a fair chance to prove itself, is one that God wants us to accept. If we're analytical by nature, we must be especially cautious not to write off a good opportunity because of its imperfections. In order to recognize God's best options for us, we will likely need to modify our expectations.

At the same time, we should remember that God brings along certain golden opportunities for their educational value, to help us better refine our vision for taking a different path. We aren't obligated to go through an open door, and if a prospect truly fails to match our potential well, we are free to disregard it.

Take the case of Harrison. He is thirty and has long wished to be married. For three years he has dated Alicia, who longs to marry him. He has leaned toward marrying her for much of this time, too, and sees many strong points in their relationship. Yet he has also wavered at times, wondering whether he might find someone more perfectly suited for him if he waited longer. The fact that God has allowed him to tie up such a substantial portion of his life in this relationship, though, given his desire to be married, is significant in itself. He should put the burden of proof on why he shouldn't marry Alicia, rather than on why he should. In other words, apart from a compelling reason not to marry, he should go ahead.

Suppose, though, that Harrison lacks the desire to be married to begin with, and is confident he would be happier staying single. No opportunity to marry—no matter how wonderful—should convince him to get married in this case.

Expectant Freedom

We have, in short, an extraordinary basis for confidence and hope as we pursue our goals and dreams, and weigh various alternatives that we face. If Christ is Lord of my life, I may assume he'll be providing me with important opportunities to employ my gifts and to realize the desires he has placed in my heart. This conviction should add a note of anticipation to each day—that on any given day, options may arise that will forever affect my destiny in a positive way. My default assumption should be that a good opportunity is Christ's provision for my needs and his way of prodding me ahead.

Yet I'm also free to weigh each prospect that comes along, and am not obliged to any conclusion about God's will until I've done so. In some cases, I'll find that even an exceptional opportunity isn't right for me, but is God's way of helping me recognize that another option fits me better.

Call this perspective on open doors "expectant freedom," if you will. It means good news for us as Christians, as we live each day and confront each opportunity.

More than anything, we should take great encouragement in knowing that God will enable us to resolve even our most difficult choices, when we ask for his direction. This is the most enlightening insight we learn from Jesus' surprising decision to turn away from the harvest opportunity in Capernaum. He was *praying,* in the early morning, at that time; it was through prayer that he gained the clarity of mind to make this complicated choice (Mk 1:35). We're reminded of our critical need to prayerfully seek God's leading when we're facing a challenging decision. And we're shown that he may be trusted fully to guide us when we do.

Our need for his guidance is never greater than on those occasions when we face golden opportunities that don't seem quite right for us. Yet we may approach these decisions with unspeakable confidence that Christ will give us exactly the insight we need to resolve them successfully—when we open ourselves to his help.

To say it in the most positive possible way: His availability to guide us, and his willingness to do so, is unceasing. This is the best news. That door is always open.

*   *   *   *   *   *   *   *

Of course, to speak of prayer at all brings us to another matter that's important to consider in this book. For prayer involves not only asking for guidance, but a whole range of communication with God, including confession, thanksgiving, praise—and *petition*—that is, asking for God's help and provision for our needs. We've been stressing the importance of taking personal initiative as Christians, when we have the chance to do something productive toward solving a problem, meeting a need we have, or moving toward a goal or dream. We should be strongly committed to keeping our life in motion, when there's something at least potentially helpful we can do toward these ends (chapter three). But we also need to think long-term, and avoid diversions to the important goals and dreams God inspires in us, as we've just been discussing.

But what is our responsibility to pray for God's help in this process—not only in determining what to do, but in asking him to prosper our efforts and provide our needs? Such praying is, indeed, a vital part of the initiative, the "action" we're expected to take as Christians in living responsibly. And so how does wait-or-initiate apply here? Once we've raised a concern to God, should we simply leave the matter in his hands and not bother him further with our request? Or are we expected to continuing praying until he answers? And should we make such prayers of petition boldly, or only provisionally ("if it be your will")? We'll look at these questions in the next chapter.

5

Am I Praying in God's Will or Against It?

WHEN PRAYING FOR PERSONAL CONCERNS, two questions often confuse us. One is how long to persist in making a request to God. Do we reach a point when persevering in prayer amounts to pushing God and refusing to accept his will? When does persistent praying indicate *faith,* and when *stubbornness?*

The second question is how boldly we should frame our requests to God. Should we straightforwardly tell him what we wish him to do, and leave it at that? Or should we pray only provisionally, saying, "Lord, *if it be your will,* please answer this request"?

Marilyn is one of many I've known who have wrestled with the persistence question. She had been separated from her husband for about two years, and had prayed earnestly that God would reunite them. Since she hadn't seen results, she wondered if she was fighting God by continuing to petition in this way. "At what point should I stop praying for my desire and simply ask for acceptance of the situation?" she asked me.

I was comfortable telling Marilyn that she should continue bringing her request to God until he clearly answers yes or no. Jesus' parable of the tenacious widow seeking a judge's help (Lk 18:1-8) is a dramatic reminder that there are times when long-term persistence in prayer is not only permitted but recommended. Jesus told the parable that we might "always pray and not lose heart" (Lk 18:1). Clearly his point is that we shouldn't lose heart in praying about *specific personal concerns,* no matter how long it takes to receive an answer.

Admittedly, when no answer seems to be forthcoming, we can feel uneasy continuing to raise a request to God. We worry that we're pestering God and praying against his will. We should remember, though, that prayer not only has an effect upon God but *upon us.* Any prayer that I make—even for a purely personal desire—has the effect of putting me in communication with God. A channel is established through which he can influence my thoughts and feelings. Through continually bringing a desire to God in prayer, I actually put myself in the best position for him to change it if he wishes.

Indeed, one of the great benefits of continuing prayer is that through it our desires become clarified. Some grow stronger. Others fade away, and we're grateful God refrained from answering them!

Of course, if a desire goes against Scripture, or if God has said no to it in a clear and resolute way, praying for it is disrespectful to him. In such cases we should pray merely that God will give us a heart to accept the situation—and persist in that prayer until our heart changes. But when God hasn't plainly said no, we should not only feel freedom but a mandate to continue raising our request to him until he gives an explicit answer.

Reverence vs. Boldness

We as Christians wrestle as much with the second question—about how bold we should be in praying—as we do with the matter of persistence. I recall a retreat where I led a session on the topic of prayer. During it, a woman asked just how direct we should be in making a request for personal healing. I asked others in the group what they thought, and a spirited discussion arose. About half of those present insisted that a prayer for healing should be bold and not provisional. The rest claimed it should be made only tentatively, in the spirit of "Lord, if it is your will, please heal me."

If we've been Christian for any time at all, we've probably heard both of these perspectives taught and preached about as frequently and with equal conviction. Chances are we're left confused, wondering which is the truly right—and reverent—way to approach God in prayer.

Frankly, I see value in both of these approaches. Qualifying a prayer with "if it is your will" shows reverence and openness to God's will. Our single greatest need in the Christian life—far and away—is to seek God's will and submit to it. And our prayers to God should never be made in the spirit of demands, but as requests for a loving Father to consider. When Jesus poured out his heart to God in Gethsemane, he strongly conditioned his request with "not my will, but yours be done" (Lk 22:42).

Jesus, though, knew that what he was asking was contrary to God's will. The purpose of his prayer was to ask God to give him the courage and the heart for what he had to do. Normally when we pray, we're not in such a clear position to know if a request is against God's will; often we have strong reason to hope that our prayer is in line with what God wants. Most of the hundreds of prayers of individuals recorded in Scripture were not made in the qualified way Jesus worded his plea in Gethsemane, but much more straightforwardly.

Praying with Liberty

Actually, I believe that these perspectives reconcile in a way that is liberating to understand. *Both* have something important to contribute to our prayer life.

On the one hand, we have an ongoing, chronic need to ask God to help us to understand his will and be open to doing it. We should pray frequently that he will make our desires conform to his. Having prayed in this way, we should then feel great freedom to word our requests to God reverently but not provisionally. Especially when a desire or concern is strong, and we have no doubt that we want God to move in a certain way to meet it, we should be explicit in telling him so—not feeling that we have to footnote the prayer with "but only if it's your will."

Paul prayed in such a straightforward manner when he asked God to remove the thorn from his side (2 Cor 12:7-9). He "pleaded with the Lord" three times to take it away. His prayer wasn't provisional in any way. He *begged* God to remove the thorn, and persisted until God responded. God finally said no. "But he said to me, 'My grace is sufficient for you,'" Paul explains, and the Greek word for "said" implies a firm, irrevocable reply. At this point, Paul ceased petitioning and relished in God's answer. Still, he never indicates that he felt remorse for having prayed so fervently and unconditionally up until this point. Instead, he implies that his earnest petitioning was *appropriate*—an example of healthy praying.

Most prayers recorded in Scripture were answered yes. But I find it interesting that even Paul's prayer about the thorn, which

God answered differently than Paul desired, gives us encouragement to be bold and direct with our requests.

In praying for personal healing, too, we should remember how we approach a doctor or medical professional for help. We never qualify a request for a doctor's help with "if you wish." We wouldn't say, "Please help me find a cure for this back pain, if you're willing to do so." Rather, we would explain our need plainly to the doctor, and respectfully ask for the best help he or she is able to provide. How much more freedom should we feel to bring requests for healing boldly to the Great Physician!

We should take heart also in the fact that Jesus gave at least as much attention during his earthly ministry to healing physical and emotional wounds people experienced as he did to teaching doctrinal truth. He demonstrated vividly that it's God's nature to bring comfort—and often healing—to those who are ill. We shouldn't feel squeamish about asking God to bring healing when it's needed, to others or ourselves.

Praying with Confidence
We can relax in knowing that our prayers won't constrain God to do anything he doesn't wish to do. We are assured in Romans 8:26-27 that the Holy Spirit interprets our prayers to God according to his will. In a sense, to constantly qualify our prayers with "if it is your will" is redundant!

Not that there's anything wrong with praying in this way. I wouldn't suggest, as some would, that such language makes a prayer ineffective, by implying to God that we lack the faith he will answer it. God looks upon our heart far more than our words in considering our prayers. But if there's a problem with such wording, it's that it may lessen our enthusiasm to pray. We're most inspired to pray when we're convinced that God takes our prayers seriously. The compulsion to constantly amend our prayers with "if it is your will" may indicate that we don't believe our requests are important to God. The result may be that we pray less, thus giving God less opportunity to work within us to fashion our desires according to his will.

From beginning to end, Scripture shows a consistent pattern among God's people of plainspoken, courageous and persistent praying. In most cases, too, the prayers were remarkably effective, and demonstrate the truth of what C. S. Lewis observed—that God purposely limits much of what he chooses to do in our lives and in the world to what we care enough to *ask* him to do. We should take great encouragement from these examples that we can approach God's throne of grace with confidence, and bring our petitions boldly before him!

6

Faith and Assertiveness

OUR CONCERN IN THIS BOOK is with the role of personal initiative in the Christian life. When does God wish us to assert ourselves, and in what ways are we called to be assertive? In the first four chapters we stressed the importance of asserting *our life*—of taking steps of faith when we have the chance to do something productive toward a need or goal. In the last chapter we spoke of the importance of asserting ourselves *with God*, of raising our needs in prayer to him, reverently, but boldly and persistently, until we receive an answer.

A critical issue related to our initiative remains, and that's what our responsibility is to assert ourselves *with others* who treat us unfairly, inconsiderately or abusively—what we may call assertiveness in the most conventional sense. Since Jesus spoke so forcefully of "turning the other cheek," are we expected to stay silent on these occasions, to let the mistreatment continue, and to leave our vindication solely in God's hands? Or are there occasions when we're responsible to speak our mind, and to take decisive action to stop unfairness or abuse that we're suffering?

How to Love an Inconsiderate Friend?

It's 10:30 Saturday evening and Susan's phone rings. Wanting to ignore it, she lets it ring four times, then out of guilt picks it up. "Hi, how are you? This is Pat," a woman's voice announces. Before Susan can respond, Pat continues, "Hon, I know this is asking a lot, but could you pick me up at the bus station and drive me home? I just got in from San Diego."

"Do you have the money for a taxi?" Susan asks. "If I have to," Pat responds. "But you know, Christmas is only a month away, and I really need to conserve . . ."

Susan, already worn out, still has work to do on a junior high Sunday school lesson she has to teach. The bus station is twenty minutes away, and Pat's home is on the other side of town. By the time she'd get back she'd have no energy left to prepare. Besides, Pat has taken advantage of her more times than Susan can remember.

Susan would like to tell Pat she has neither the time nor the energy to come for her. And, when she can collect herself, she would like to speak honestly with Pat about her presumptuousness. Yet Susan remembers Jesus' admonition to go the second mile. "Isn't this clearly a situation where I need to bend for someone else?" she wonders. "Wouldn't confronting Pat violate Jesus' command to turn the other cheek? Doesn't God require me to deny myself for Pat's sake?"

The Ongoing Question

To assert yourself or not to do so? To stand up for yourself or go along with someone else's wishes? We struggle with this issue often as Christians. For Susan, the question is whether to cave in to a friend's unreasonable expectations. Like her, we each face situations where people try to take advantage of us—occasions when friends expect too much of us, for instance, or when someone in business tries to exploit us. The sensitive Christian wonders, "Should I stand up for my rights—or is it more godly to give in?"

In other cases our concern isn't with standing up for our rights but with whether to express ourselves straightforwardly. Should I speak up and say what I'm thinking in this class? Should I tell her how much I care for her? Should I share my faith with him? Should I state my qualifications confidently in this job interview?

Many of us are uncomfortable asserting ourselves in some situations, and some of us in any setting. One problem may be that we're shy or feel awkward with people. We fear we'll fail in our attempt to be outspoken and experience unbearable embarrassment. Learning how to confront and manage our fears is a major step forward in becoming more assertive. We need to strive, too, for greater optimism about our possibilities for success.

Yet we're often hindered as well by misconceptions about biblical teaching. We assume that being assertive implies behavior that is patently unchristian: demanding our rights, trampling over the needs of others and feeling the freedom to blow our lid whenever we feel like it.

Healthy Assertiveness

Most writers and teachers who promote assertiveness have two goals. One is to help individuals "own" their own lives—to break free of the control of others' expectations and to stay in control of their emotions when they speak. If I ventilate anger at others, for example, it suggests that I'm not being freely assertive but am letting their expectations control me, for I've allowed them to upset me. Owning my own life is more likely reflected in my responding calmly, even politely to them. Thus the feisty Manuel J. Smith, author of a best-selling book on assertiveness, devotes a surprising portion to helping readers learn to accept criticism graciously and nondefensively.[1]

The other aim of assertiveness training is to encourage individuals to take initiative to express their convictions and concerns honestly to others. Such self-expression shouldn't be at the wholesale expense of others' feelings; indeed, assertiveness is most effective when exercised with empathy and compassion. Still, expressing yourself is important. It contributes not only to your own well-being and productivity, but to the quality of your relationships as well.

When defined this way, assertiveness is not incompatible with Paul's instruction to speak the truth in love to each other in Ephesians 4:15. There, he clearly admonishes Christians to be assertive, at least within certain boundaries.

Still, we may be more inclined to think of the boundaries than of the freedom or mandate implied in any biblical teaching on assertiveness. And the notion of owning our life, at the heart of assertiveness training, seems to fly in the face of what we've long been taught—that we must sacrifice our interests for others' needs. Can such unselfishness possibly reconcile with owning our life?

Owning Your Life

In fact it can, and the two concepts go hand in hand in Scripture. In the biblical understanding, I am called to give myself to another's needs as an act of free will. It's this free-choice aspect of my decision to help another that makes it a true response of Christian compassion. Yet I can only give myself freely if I own my life in the first place.

It's in this spirit that Paul declares, "Though I am free and belong to no man, I make myself a slave to everyone, to win as many as possible" (1 Cor 9:19). Here and elsewhere Paul emphasizes about equally his cherished liberty as a child of Christ and his deliberate decision to invest his life for the sake of others. Because he is free to begin with, he can make the choice to sacrifice for others from compassion and healthy motivation.

When we look for it, in fact, we find this assumption implicit whenever the Scriptures urge us to give ourselves to the needs of others: we must first own our own lives. It is there, for instance, in various descriptions of Jesus himself. He was able to wash his disciples' feet because of the strong sense of identity he had in the first place: "Jesus, knowing that the Father had given all things into his hands, and that he had come from God and was going to God, rose from supper, laid aside his garments, and girded himself with a towel. Then he poured water into a basin, and began to wash the disciples' feet" (Jn 13:3-5 RSV).

It is there, too, where we might least expect it—in Jesus' teaching about turning the other cheek in his Sermon on the Mount. There he cautions against a retributive spirit, and mentions three occasions where we should give double compliance to an aggressor:

"You have heard that it was said, 'Eye for eye, and tooth for tooth.' But I tell you, Do not resist an evil person. If someone strikes you on the right cheek, turn to him the other also. And if someone wants to sue you and take your tunic, let him have your cloak as well. If someone forces you to go one mile, go with him two miles. Give to the one who asks you, and do not turn away from the one who wants to borrow from you." (Mt 5:38-42)

It might seem that Jesus was exhorting us to be a doormat to others' aggression and abuse, and many Christians have taken his teaching in exactly this way. This is certainly the last thing Jesus meant. Rather, by urging double compliance, he was telling us to *take control* of an unjust situation.

By choosing to walk a second mile with someone, instead of the single mile they demand, I demonstrate that I am deciding for myself what my response will be. From this angle, going the second mile and turning the other cheek are profoundly assertive acts. Such double compliance also aims to have two redemptive effects on the other person. It shows him I will not let him manipulate me, and perhaps erases his desire to do so. It also shames her for her decision to take advantage of me.

Considering the Outcome
This perspective is truly liberating, for it suggests that if turning the other cheek will not affect another redemptively, or will result in someone's harm, I'm not expected to respond in this way. Certain Christian men during the Russian revolution who stood by and allowed soldiers to rape their wives, believed they were fulfilling Jesus' requirement for passivity yet seriously misunderstood his intent.

Numerous unjust situations occur where we benefit no one by complying with the injury or by rolling over and playing dead. A woman whose husband abuses her helps neither him nor herself by allowing him to treat her cruelly.

In the same way, I am usually kidding myself if I think that any positive Christian witness results from allowing someone in a modern business situation to cheat me financially. An impersonal climate exists in most business transactions today that renders turning the other cheek ineffective.

If a car dealership performs shoddy repairs on my car, for instance, I help no one in their spiritual journey by choosing not to complain. Employees won't likely connect my silence with my

Christian convictions. The proper Christian response in this case is to point out the problem to them and to calmly but persistently insist that they make the proper repair—for by doing so, I'm denting their conviction that they can take advantage of their customers.

Does the Shoe Fit?

I also doubt that Jesus meant to lay the mandate of turning the other cheek upon all believers at all stages in their spiritual development. He gave this instruction to his "disciples" (Mt 5:1)—that is, to those who were at a stage of growth where they were ready to respond to others at this level.

Not once in the Gospels, for instance, did Jesus preach self-denial or the need for noble sacrifice to someone who was physically or emotionally ill. Instead—and without exception—he healed the sick or needy person and did not immediately lay the burden of moving mountains upon him or her. It was to those who were well, in body and mind, that Jesus urged self-denial. They were able to give themselves to others for his sake because they had a self to give.

There is, in short, a developmental process in becoming assertive that accords fully with biblical teaching. Turning the other cheek is the ideal. Yet we must be honest with ourselves about whether we're ready to do it in a healthy manner. If you're shy, you've probably found it difficult to stand up for yourself and to make independent decisions. Allow yourself time to grow and to learn to own your life more fully. Then, when you can truly do it freely, be open to those special instances when Christ may call you to turn the other cheek. Focus first upon becoming more assertive, as part of taking responsible stewardship of your life as a Christian.

One other point is helpful to keep in mind in turning-the-other-cheek situations. As my friend Omar Omland points out in his inspiring book *The Third Mile,* Jesus spoke of double compliance in certain situations, but never of triple compliance.[2] While he encouraged the second mile, he didn't necessarily recommend a third. There may be limits, then, to how fully he expects us to sacrifice in order to help someone. In every case the vital matter is that we give ourselves *freely.* We're called first to own our life, then to respond to others' needs in light of the energy God gives us and the priorities he lays upon us.

7

Embracing Initiative

I HOPE THAT OUR DISCUSSION in this brief book has freed you up in some important ways. I hope you're feeling greater liberty to take steps of faith to solve certain problems you face, or to meet certain needs you have. I hope also that you're feeling more optimistic about resolving decisions and finding solutions your problems—even vexing ones—and that you're more motivated to look earnestly and creatively for the answers. I hope, too, that you're feeling more permission to persist in raising certain requests to God through prayer, and more comfortable asserting yourself with others when it's recommended. Most of all, I hope you're feeling inspired to better understand how God has gifted and motivated you, and to embrace goals and dreams that move you forward toward his best options for your life.

Both my personal experience and more than forty-five years

of counseling others have impressed on me, time and again, that we Christians instinctively feel uneasy taking initiatives such as these—for we fear pushing God's hand and taking matters too greatly into our own. While this fear is often reverent and well-intentioned, it misses the fact that living by faith involves stepping out in faith every bit as much as passively waiting. And, so often, by taking prayerful but bold initiative, we compel ourselves to greater faith than comes by merely sitting still—for we oblige ourselves to trust more fully in Christ to protect and provide for us. And as we embrace life's bigger adventures by taking action, we still encounter plenty of obstacles that require us to wait patiently for him to provide. And so stepping out in faith often leads to our best opportunities to wait in faith and learn patience.

In concluding, I urge you not only to approach life more proactively, but to strive to think *big* about your future. We're happiest, most productive and helpful to others, when we're pursuing goals and dreams that tap our best potential, and inspire us to new horizons. During the lifetime Christ entrusts to each of us, he provides us generous time to harvest our gifts, further his mission, and make our best contribution to others' needs. Yet it is also limited time, and so we must manage it wisely. To this end we must not "play it safe" nor be risk-adverse. Realizing our potential for Christ requires us to take certain steps that from our standpoint seem risky. Yet, again, they're exactly what position us to trust more fully in him—*and* enjoy his greater blessings.

Generally, we best determine what steps God wants us to take by understanding how he has made us—the gifts and desires most generic to our personality—then striving to match these with the best opportunities to serve available. To this end, we need to think long-term, and embrace goals and dreams most likely to move us in God's best directions for us.

I encourage you to think expansively about your future, and to muse optimistically about the possibilities. What changes in your life would you most like to see one year from now? In five years? Ten? If you're single, would you like to be married? Are you eager to find a job or career that better fits your talents? Do you long for a certain mission or ministry, or role in your church, that fits naturally with who you are? Are you inspired to develop a certain talent or ability for which you're obviously gifted? Do you want to live in a different part of America or the world? Do you wish for a major lifestyle change?

Ponder possibilities like these, and see if a clear vision for your future emerges. Then allow yourself some quality time—a personal retreat, if possible—and map out strategy for getting there. Then begin moving toward your dream(s), one step at a time. This sort of musing, planning and moving forward is at the heart of what stepping out in faith involves.

If you'd like further help with goal setting and achieving personal dreams, I have a full-length book on the subject: *Reach Beyond Your Grasp: Embracing Dreams That Reflect God's Best for You—And Achieving Them*, plus a shorter one, *Goal Setting for the Christian*. If you're single wanting to be married, I offer advice for reaching that dream in *Marry a Friend: Finding Someone to Marry Who Is Truly Right for You*. All of my other books also deal with different aspects of realizing our potential as Christians.

More than anything, though, I encourage you to heed the advice of chapter three of this book, and commit yourself to a lifestyle of keeping your life in motion. For even when you're uncertain what to do, your subconscious is working for you, and—most important—God is guiding your decision process. And so by staying in motion, you sometimes compel choices that, even though made less than confidently, prove highly fortu-itous. Happy surprises are far more likely when you're active than sitting still.

I think of two very talented young men I know who have had vastly different experiences with job seeking. One has been stuck for some time in a low-paying job well beneath his potential. Con-vinced that "the job market isn't good," he has looked only half-heartedly for better employment. The other also held an unsatisfying job, yet decided to take steps which *to me* seemed overly risky—including multiple interviews requiring time off from work and the possibility his boss would detect his search for greener pastures. Yet in the end he received three job offers, all substantial improvements on his current position.

Of course, there are a multitude of factors that affect our success or failure in job seeking, and which may have given the one young man better fortune than the other. But almost always it requires *effort* on our part, stepping out in faith boldly rather than merely waiting, and pushing through plenty of rejection and dis-couragement in the process.

I think also of a friend well into her adult years who dearly wants to be married, but has hit more dead ends than she or I can possibly begin to count. Yet this past year she tried yet again, through an online service, and now is enjoying a remarkably good relationship that will likely end in marriage. Staying in motion has made a world of difference for her.

It can make a significant difference for you as well. Treat the Christian life as a grand adventure—which is surely what Jesus meant when he promised us "abundant life"—and commit your-self to taking steps of faith that reflect this energized spirit. Take the time to establish goals and dreams that reflect God's best for your life, and then err on the side of action, persistence and cour-age in reaching them. And when you're uncertain what to do, or your options seem limited, tilt toward doing something rather than nothing. Position yourself for welcome surprises, and God's doing the unexpected.

I wish you every blessing of the Lord as you seek to realize your highest potential for him, and those vital aspirations he inspires within you!

Notes

Chapter 2: The Eureka Factor
[1]Wolfgang Köhler, Max Wertheimer, and Kurt Koffka were the pioneers and main proponents of Gestalt psychology.
[2] Amy Lowell, "The Process of Making Poetry," in *The Creative Process*, edited by Brewster Ghiselin (New York: Mentor Books, 1952) pp. 109-110.
[3]Although Isaiah heard God's voice in the temple saying, "Whom shall I send?," he reached his own conclusion that it was right for him personally to respond. Paul's dream of the man in Macedonia (described as a "vision" in most English translations) may have been a direct revelation from God; however, Paul never found a man in ministry in Macedonia once he ventured there, but a Jewish woman (Lydia) whom he converted, and who became pivotal to his ministry in that region. Given these circumstances, it's likely Paul's night-vision was a dream, and part of his normal gestalt process in deciding to travel to Macedonia.

Chapter 6: Faith and Assertiveness
[1]Manuel J. Smith, *When I Say No, I Feel Guilty* (New York: Dial Press, 1975).
[2]Omar K. Omland, *The Third Mile: A Biblical View of Codependency* (Fergus Falls, Minn.: Faith and Fellowship Press, 1992).

About the Author

Blaine Smith, a Presbyterian pastor, spent thirty years as director of Nehemiah Ministries, Inc., a resource ministry based in the Washington, D.C. area. He retired the organization in 2009, but continues to use the name Nehemiah Ministries for free-lance work.

His career has included giving seminars and lectures, speaking at conferences, counseling, and writing. He is author of ten books, including *Marry a Friend, Knowing God's Will* (original and revised editions), *Should I Get Married?* (original and revised editions), *The Yes Anxiety, Overcoming Shyness, Faith and Optimism* (originally *The Optimism Factor), One of a Kind, Reach Beyond Your Grasp, Emotional Intelligence for Christians, Goal Setting for the Christian*, as well as numerous articles. These books have been published in more than thirty English language and international editions. He is also lecturer for *Guidance By The Book*, a home study course with audio cassettes produced by the Christian Broadcasting Network as part of their *Living By The Book* series.

Blaine served previously as founder/director of the Sons of Thunder, believed by many to be America's first active Christian rock band, and as assistant pastor of Memorial Presbyterian Church in St. Louis. He is an avid guitarist, and currently performs with the Newports, an oldies band.

Blaine is a graduate of Georgetown University, and also holds a Master of Divinity from Wesley Theological Seminary and a Doctor of Ministry from Fuller Theological Seminary. He and Evie live in Gaithersburg, Maryland. They've been married since 1973, and have two grown sons, Benjamin and Nathan. Ben and his wife Lorinda have two children, Jackson Olen (2009) and Marlena Mae (2012).

Blaine also authors a twice-monthly online newsletter, *Nehemiah Notes*, featuring a practical article on the Christian faith, posted on his ministry website and available by e-mail for free.

You may e-mail Blaine at mbs@nehemiahministries.com.

www.ingramcontent.com/pod-product-compliance
Lightning Source LLC
Chambersburg PA
CBHW060707030426
42337CB00017B/2790